THE MYSTERY OF THE HIEROGLYPHS

THE STORY OF THE ROSETTA STONE AND THE RACE TO DECIPHER EGYPTIAN HIEROGLYPHS

CAROL DONOUGHUE

NEW YORK

OXFORD UNIVERSITY PRESS

This book is dedicated to the teacher and pupils of Ashurstwood Primary School who gave me such good advice, and to all my children.

© 1999 Carol Donoughue
Carol Donoughue has asserted her right to be identified as the author of this work.

Published in the United States of America by
Oxford University Press, Inc.
198 Madison Avenue, New York, New York 10016

Oxford is a registered trademark of Oxford University Press, Inc.

ISBN 0-19-521553-2 (lib. ed.); ISBN 0-19-521554-0 (trade ed.)

First published in 1999 by British Museum Press,
A division of The British Museum Company Limited,
46 Bloomsbury Street, London WC1B 3QQ

Designed by Peartree Design. Printed and bound in Singapore by Imago
9 8 7 6 5 4 3 2

Illustration acknowledgments
All the hieroglyphs, the maps and the illustrations on pp. 9, 21 and 41 were drawn by Claire Thorne. The illustration on p. 8 top was drawn by Richard Parkinson.

Photographs
© Lesley and Roy Adkins Picture Library p. 37; Agence photographique de la réunion des musées nationaux, p. 30 top; Ashmolean Museum, Oxford p. 11 left; Bibliothèque Municipale de Grenoble, p. 31; © The British Museum pp. 4, 5, 6, 7, 8 top, 9 top and centre, 10 top, 10 below (photo Graham Harrison), 12 (photo Graham Harrison), 13 (photo Graham Harrison), 15, 18 below (photo Graham Harrison), 19 top (photo Graham Harrison), 20 below, 22, 23, 24, 25, 27, 29, 32 centre (photo Graham Harrison), 33, 34, 35, 43; © Maurice et Pierre Chuzeville/Musée du Louvre p. 8 below; Holt Studios Photographic Library, p. 9 below; Museo Archeologico, Firenze p. 11 top; Museé Champollion, Figeac, p. 30 below (photo Nelly Blaya), 36, 39 left, 39 right (photo Ms. Chotard-Vasseur); © National Gallery London, portrait of Napoleon by Vernet, p. 20 top; © SCALA, painting by Angelelli Giuseppi, *Spedizione franco-toscana in Egitto*, in Museo Archeologico, Firenze p.38.

CONTENTS

If a word is printed in **bold type** you can look up what it means in the Glossary on pages 46-47.

HOW THE EGYPTIANS WROTE

If you ever visit the British Museum in London you will find, in the Egyptian Sculpture Gallery, a large dark grey stone. There is always a crowd of people standing and staring at the stone. Quite often there is a museum guide talking about the stone to a group of visitors. Why do so many people come to look at this large stone?

The Rosetta Stone

The Rosetta Stone turned out to be the most important clue to the mystery which had been puzzling **historians** since the time of the Greeks and the Romans: how to read the writing covering the statues and temples and mummy cases which had been found amongst the ruins of Ancient Egypt. The Stone was found in Egypt two hundred years ago in 1799, but if you look at the timeline on pages 12-17, you will see that some Egyptians had carved it and written on it and set it up for people to see in 196 BC, almost two thousand years before. It is called the Rosetta Stone because it was found in a place that was called Rosetta.

Now that we can understand the writing, we know that it describes how the young King Ptolemy V of Egypt, who had been on the throne for nine years, had passed laws to give more money to the **priests** and that in return the priests had decided to build statues of Ptolemy in all the temples and to worship the statues three times a day.

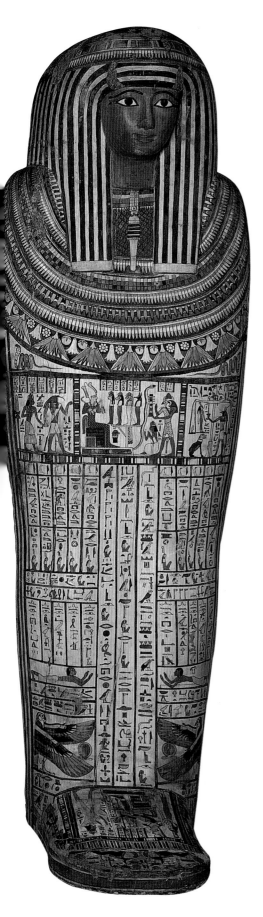

There are three different kinds of writing (or **script**) on the Stone, and you can see that none of it is in English, nor is it written in the alphabet that we use. What makes it so interesting to all those visitors at the British Museum is that the writing on the top part of the stone looks like lines of small pictures.

It was only after 1822, when a Frenchman called Jean François Champollion began to understand what the pictures meant, that historians were able to read the Ancient Egyptian writing. Until that time they had been able to guess how the Ancient Egyptians lived by looking at the paintings and carvings on the walls of tombs and temples, or on mummy cases, or on rolls of papyrus, but they could not be certain that they were right. It was like looking through a book with illustrations, but not being able to read the words. It was like a secret code. They had tried and tried to **decipher** the hieroglyphic writing, but they had never managed to read or understand it. If the Rosetta Stone had not been discovered it would have taken much longer to work out what the writing meant.

But once it was possible to understand the writing, then the mystery was solved! Now, if you have learned to read this strange writing, you can walk around all the other objects in the Egyptian Galleries in the British Museum and other museums and find out what was written by the Egyptian scribes thousands of years ago. But it is not so easy to learn to read Ancient Egyptian, as you will see!

5

In this book you will find the story of the Rosetta Stone and learn how to read some of the hieroglyphs – which is what the pictures are called. But first, look again at the writing on the stone, both at the top section and at the different writing underneath it. We know now that both pieces of writing say the same thing. They are both written in the Egyptian language but in different scripts, in the same way that you might see the words ROSETTA STONE written like this:

ROSETTA STONE

or like this:

Rosetta Stone

The hieroglyphs – or the hieroglyphic script – were often carved on walls or slabs of stone, like the Rosetta Stone. They were particularly used by the Egyptian priests, who called this writing 'the writing of the divine words'.

The second script that you see on the Stone is now known as the 'demotic' script. It was used for everyday writing – for business letters or books about medicine, for example.

HIEROGLYPHIC SCRIPT

Hieroglyph means 'sacred carving'. It is how the Greeks described the writing used by the Ancient Egyptian priests.

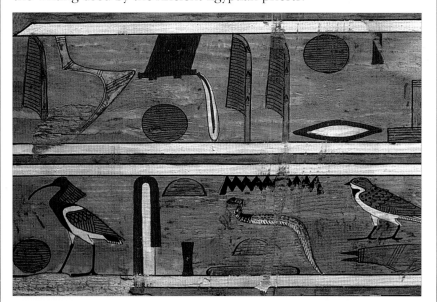

Hieroglyphs painted on an Egyptian coffin.

DEMOTIC SCRIPT

Demotic means 'popular'. It is how the Greeks described the everyday writing used by Egyptians after the seventh century BC.

The third section of the Stone is written in **Greek**. By 196 BC a Greek family called the Ptolemies had been ruling Egypt for over a hundred years, so the Greek alphabet and language was being used in Egypt alongside Egyptian writing. Can you see how different it looks from the Egyptian writing?

The same words were written in the three different scripts so that anyone who could read could understand what they meant – Egyptians and Greeks alike. This really meant the priests and officials - very few ordinary people could read at all.

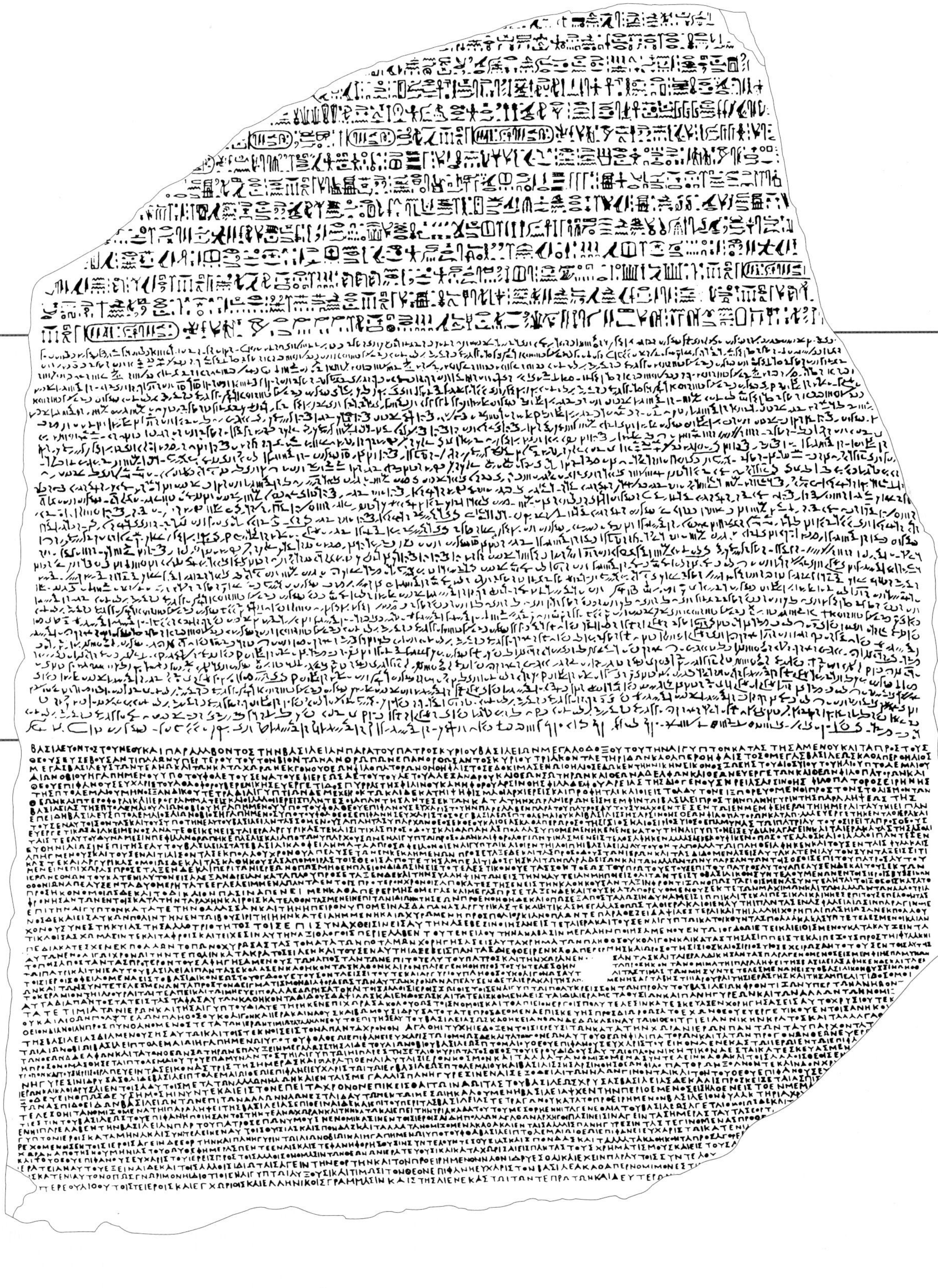

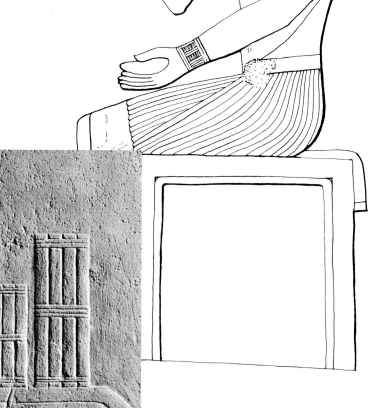

How did they write on stone? To begin with, a scribe, or writer, drew or painted the signs on to the stone and then a **sculptor** carved the shape of the signs into the stone.

Look at this picture. →

What is he using? Do you think it would have been easy to write like this?

← If you look at this picture you will see that scribes did not always write on stone.

What is the scribe doing here? What is he writing on? What is he using to write with?

SCRIBE

A scribe was someone who could write. He wrote down what people said, or copied writing. In ancient times most people who wanted something written down asked a scribe to write it for them, because they did not know how. Only a few people learned to write.

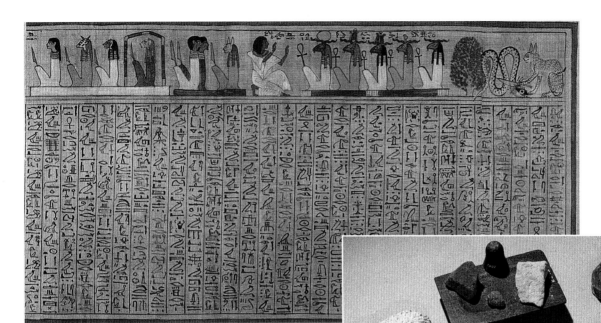

Look at the photographs of a papyrus scroll, ↑ and of a scribe's palette, inks and brushes. →

By looking at them we can tell how the scribe wrote. Of course, if you are writing with a brush on papyrus, you can write faster than if you are chiselling into stone.

PAPYRUS

Papyrus is the name of a reed used by the Ancient Egyptians for making a kind of paper. They sliced the stem into thin slices and laid some lengthwise and others across them. Then they moistened the layers with water, pressed them with a heavy weight and dried them. When they were dry, the layers stuck together in a sheet. The sheet was rubbed smooth and then it was ready to be used to write on. The sheets were joined together into rolls, some of which were very long indeed – up to 40 metres long.

Now look at this. It's called an ostracon. The writing on it looks like a rough sketch doesn't it? Perhaps it was done by a scribe practising drawing a duck hieroglyph, before he started on the real thing, or a young boy, learning how to write that particular hieroglyph.

OSTRACON

An ostracon is a small flake of stone or a piece of broken pottery. Scribes used ostraca in the same way as you use a rough book, to practise writing something or to sketch a drawing.

Carving of the female Pharaoh, Hatshepsut, surrounded by hieroglyphs.

Have you noticed anything else about the hieroglyphic **script** and the demotic script? Look at the page you are reading in this book and then look again at the papyrus scroll and the Rosetta Stone. In the Egyptian writing there are no gaps between words, so it is impossible to tell where one word ends and another begins, whichmakesitvery difficulttoreadparticularlyifyoucannotunderstandwhatthesignsmean.

There are no full stops or commas and there are no paragraphs. You could try copying out some of this page without putting in any of the punctuation, and see whether it makes it easier or more difficult to read.

Another difference which you may not have noticed is that the hieroglyphs are sometimes written from left to right like the writing you are reading here, but sometimes they are written from right to left: **ƨIHT ƎʞI⅃** . Sometimes they are written downwards, in columns:

L	T		T	⌐
I	H	or even	H	I
K	I		ʞ	I
E	S		ƨ	Ǝ

The scribe fitted the writing around the picture he was describing.

Now that historians can read the Egyptian scripts we know that the scribe who wrote on the Rosetta Stone would have been one of very few people in Ancient Egypt who could read and write. None of the pictures of scribes show that girls or women could write. Young boys went to a kind of primary school to learn to read and write and spent most of their time there copying lines of writing from long rolls of papyrus. They often made mistakes!

Trainee scribes writing from dictation. →

This ostracon contains a very badly-copied version of a famous Egyptian story. ↓

The boys had to learn how to prepare their pens, which were made from reeds. They would cut and soften one end of the reed, then put it into water – like you do with a paintbrush – and then rub it over the cakes of colour on a palette, usually black or red. They had to learn how to sit with a long roll of papyrus, unrolling it with their left hands gradually as they wrote with their right hands, as you can see in the picture above. It can't have been very easy to do, and the boys were punished if they did not work hard enough! One teacher wrote: 'A boy's ears are on his back; he listens when he is beaten.'

When the boys were older they were given special documents to copy. These documents would have difficult words in them, and sometimes there would be foreign names to make it even more difficult.

Can you see where the teacher has corrected the mistakes on this ← papyrus?

Although it was very hard work training to become a scribe, it was considered to be a very important job and there was always work to do.

HOW WE KNOW

A map of
Ancient Egypt

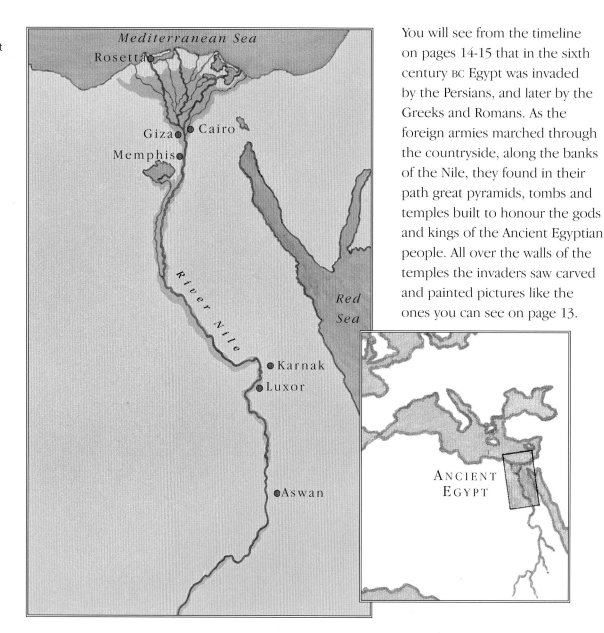

Mediterranean Sea

Rosetta

Giza Cairo

Memphis

River Nile

Red
Sea

Karnak

Luxor

Aswan

ANCIENT
EGYPT

You will see from the timeline on pages 14-15 that in the sixth century BC Egypt was invaded by the Persians, and later by the Greeks and Romans. As the foreign armies marched through the countryside, along the banks of the Nile, they found in their path great pyramids, tombs and temples built to honour the gods and kings of the Ancient Egyptian people. All over the walls of the temples the invaders saw carved and painted pictures like the ones you can see on page 13.

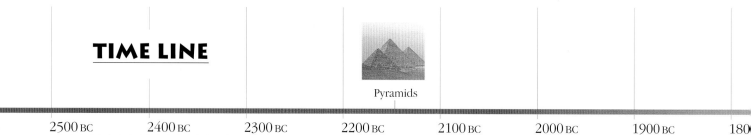

TIME LINE

Pyramids

2500 BC   2400 BC   2300 BC   2200 BC   2100 BC   2000 BC   1900 BC   180

Wall carving of Rameses II in his chariot from the Great Temple at Abu Simbel.

Around the pictures, above them, below them, and sometimes included within the picture, were signs like this:

But what did they mean? If only it were possible to work it out! Because they found the signs mainly in temples or burial places, the invaders believed that they were special sacred signs with magic powers. Would it ever be possible to read what they said?

What would you do, if you found something written down in signs which you just could not understand? How would you set about working out what the signs meant? What about these signs for instance? Any ideas?

Look carefully and see if you notice anything about them.

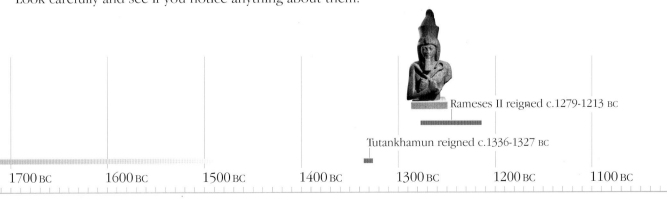

Rameses II reigned c.1279-1213 BC

Tutankhamun reigned c.1336-1327 BC

| 1700 BC | 1600 BC | 1500 BC | 1400 BC | 1300 BC | 1200 BC | 1100 BC | 1000 BC |

In the first century BC a Greek writer called Diodorus of Sicily went to Egypt. He too was fascinated by the strange and beautiful signs that surrounded the pictures. The signs were themselves small pictures, but it was clear that they were telling the story of the bigger ones. He looked carefully at the hieroglyphs and wrote about them when he got home. He wrote, 'The signs are like various animals, or the extremities of the human body, or tools – particularly carpenters' tools'.

Have a look at these hieroglyphs.

Do you agree with his description?

Diodorus used the Greek alphabet when he wrote. The ancient Greek alphabet looked like this:

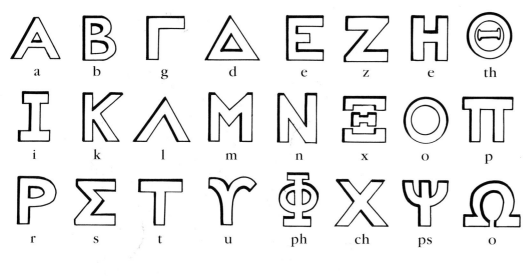

In the English alphabet and the Greek alphabet the letters stand for different sounds. Some of the letters in our alphabet are called **vowels** – a, e, i, o, u are vowels. The rest of the letters are called **consonants** – for example, b, c, d, f, g, h are all consonants. When we learn to read our alphabet, we learn the sound of each letter or group of letters, so that when we come to a word we haven't seen before we can work out how to say it by sounding it out.

Alexander the Great conquered Egypt 332 BC

Persians invaded Egypt 6th century BC

1000 BC   900 BC   800 BC   700 BC   600 BC   500 BC   400 BC   300

Diodorus made a terrible mistake. He decided that the hieroglyphic signs did not stand for sounds. What else could they stand for? Did they stand for the objects which they looked like, or for ideas, or even for syllables? Diodorus thought that each of the signs stood for an idea or a thing, and that you had to remember what the idea or thing was to be able to understand the meaning of the sign. So, for instance, he thought that this sign stood for an owl – or maybe for wisdom, because owls are meant to be wise.

Five hundred years after Diodorus, a priest called Horapollo wrote a book in Greek called *Hieroglyphika*. By that time many of the Egyptians themselves could not always read hieroglyphs without making mistakes. In the book, Horapollo said that the hieroglyphs stood for an idea or an object, but he decided that understanding the meaning of the signs was even more difficult than Diodorus had believed. He thought that each sign, or hieroglyph, sometimes had more than one meaning. He wrote,

'When they mean a mother, a sight, or boundaries or foreknowledge … they draw a vulture. A mother, since there is no male in this species of animal … the vulture stands for sight since of all other animals the vulture has the keenest vision …'

That made everything much more complicated. We now know that neither Horapollo nor Diodorus was completely wrong because some of the signs did stand for things or ideas, but mostly they stand for SOUNDS. For instance, the owl sign stands for the sound of the consonant 'm'.

Through the centuries that followed, various **scholars** tried to break the code. Because they wrote down the work they had done on breaking the code, it was possible for scholars in later times to read and use what had been discovered or even to disagree with what was written, as sometimes happened.

This hieroglyph of an owl stands for the sound 'm'.

■ Rosetta Stone 196 BC   ■ Birth of Christ

▬▬ Cleopatra reigned 51-30 BC

)lemy V reigned 205-180 BC   ▬▬▬ Diodorus of Sicily visited Egypt mid first century BC

▬▬▬   ■ Romans conquered Egypt 30 BC

| 200 BC | 100 BC | 0 | 100 AD | 200 AD | 300 AD | 400 AD | 500 AD |

Up until the eighteenth century almost all these scholars believed, like Diodorus, that the signs stood for an idea or a thing. So all they could do was guess at what the little pictures meant.

Can you imagine how difficult that was? Try to guess what this group of hieroglyphs might mean. Don't look at the translation yet!

Have you made up something about a lion and birds? What did you think the feather and the hand meant?

Now look at what it really says:

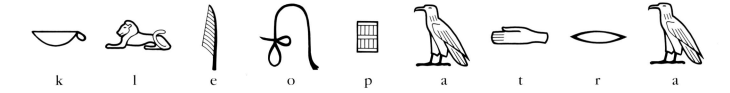

| k | l | e | o | p | a | t | r | a |

These hieroglyphs make up the sounds of the name Cleopatra.

But this sign  means 'female', because Cleopatra was a queen and not a king. It also means 'divine' or 'goddess'.

The Egyptians believed that their kings and queens were gods.

The line around the outside of the name is called a cartouche. It shows that the word is the name of a royal person.

It would be very easy to get the wrong meaning if you thought that all the signs stood for objects, as you have just found out! No wonder the scholars were puzzled for so long.

CARTOUCHE

French scholars gave this sign the name 'cartouche'. In French it means 'cartridge'. The sign is the shape of the gun cartridges used by the French army in Egypt.

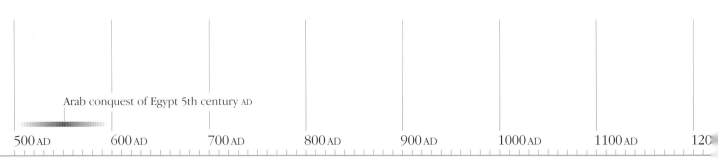

Arab conquest of Egypt 5th century AD

| 500 AD | 600 AD | 700 AD | 800 AD | 900 AD | 1000 AD | 1100 AD | 120 |

Now you have looked closely at Cleopatra's name you know that there are some signs which stand for ideas (these signs are called 'logograms'), and others which stand for sounds (these signs are called 'phonograms'). There were one or two scholars in the eighteenth century who began to work out that the hieroglyphs might contain this mixture of logograms and phonograms.

The big step forward in solving the mystery came when a Frenchman called Jean Jacques Barthélemy decided to have a good look at the hieroglyphs which were written inside the cartouches. He realized that the Egyptians put a cartouche around the name of a king or a queen like Cleopatra. Since he already knew some of the names of the Egyptian kings and queens, he began to be able to work out what the hieroglyphs stood for.

PHONOGRAMS

A phonogram is a written sign which stands for a sound. For example, in English, the letter 'l' stands for the sound which begins the word 'leaf'.

The hieroglyph ⟨lion⟩ stands for the sound 'l'.

Both the letter 'l' and the hieroglyph ⟨lion⟩ are phonograms.

LOGOGRAMS

A logogram is a written sign which stands for an object or an idea. For example, we use the sign '£' to stand for 'pounds' and '$' to stand for 'dollars'.

The hieroglyph ⟨mouth⟩ stands for 'mouth'.

The hieroglyph ⟨sun⟩ stands for 'the sun' and the name of the god Ra, but it can also stand for 'time', so it stands for an object, a name and an idea, all at the same time.

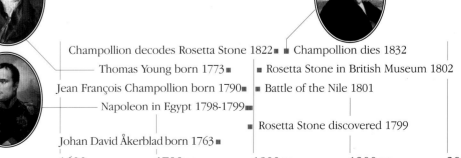

Champollion decodes Rosetta Stone 1822 ■   ■ Champollion dies 1832
Thomas Young born 1773 ■   ■ Rosetta Stone in British Museum 1802
Jean François Champollion born 1790 ■   ■ Battle of the Nile 1801
Napoleon in Egypt 1798-1799 ■
■ Rosetta Stone discovered 1799
Johan David Åkerblad born 1763 ■

1300 AD   1400 AD   1500 AD   1600 AD   1700 AD   1800 AD   1900 AD   2000 AD

Another scholar, called Johann David Åkerblad, was from Sweden. He learned the Coptic language and he guessed that Coptic might have come from ancient Egyptian. He began to work out what some of the signs in the demotic script stood for. By looking at the names of kings and queens, he managed to identify sixteen sound signs or phonograms. By 1815 he announced that he could **translate** into Coptic the collection of signs which meant month, small, man, year, victory, sun, and so on. (What he did not realize was that the Egyptians did not write most of the vowel sounds, so what he was looking at **LKD LK THS**.)

The writing on this ostracon is in Coptic.

As we saw earlier in the book, scholars had realized that there were different kinds of writing or scripts. This made things even more difficult. The script used on rolls of papyrus was often different from the script carved on to the walls of the temples. Did that mean that there was more than one Egyptian language? Or were the different scripts all used at the same time as different ways of writing down the same language?

COPTIC

The Egyptian language changed gradually over the centuries. Some of the changes were brought about because Egypt was invaded first by Persians, then by the Greeks, the Romans, the Arabs and finally the Ottoman Turks. The invaders spoke their own languages and the Egyptians learned those languages and used more and more of the words they learned.

Coptic was the latest form of the Egyptian language. It was spoken by the Egyptians during the Christian period, between the fifth and mid-seventh centuries AD. It is still used by Egyptian Christians in their church services.

The Coptic script used the letters of the Greek alphabet, but it also had seven letters which came from the Egyptian demotic script. Because most European scholars in the eighteenth and nineteenth centuries could understand and speak Greek, they were able to learn Coptic.

← Hieroglyphs carved on the back of a statue of Rameses II.

↑ Columns carved with pictures and hieroglyphs in a temple of the goddess Hathor.

BRITISH MUSEUM

Please support the Museum
All currencies welcome

El museo le agradece su apoyo.
Se aceptan todas las monedas.

Le Musee vous remercie pour votre soutien.
Nous acceptons toutes les monnaies
avec gratitude.

Unterstützen Sie das Museum.
Bitte spenden Sie.
Jede Währung willkommen.

Ogni vostro contributo sara gradito.
Qualsiasi valuta sara apprezata.

請資助博物館
歡迎各種貨幣

ご支援をお願い致します.
どの国の通貨でも結構です.

By the time the scholars in the eighteenth and nineteenth centuries were trying to answer this question, the Egyptian language (Coptic) was only used for church services and new languages like Arabic had taken over in Egypt. So the scholars had two problems. They had to try and read the ancient Egyptian writing (the script), and they had to try and understand the ancient Egyptian language.

Are you confused about the difference between a SCRIPT and a LANGUAGE? Try looking at a modern example. This Museum sign says the same thing in seven different languages. The English, Spanish, French, German and Italian are all written in the same script. You can recognize the letters of the alphabet, even if you can't understand all the languages. But the Chinese and Japanese at the bottom are written in different languages AND in completely different script.

19

THE DISCOVERY OF THE ROSETTA STONE

NAPOLEON

Napoleon (1769–1821) was a famous soldier and led the French army to victory in many famous battles in Europe. He became Emperor of the French and King of Italy. He never crossed the Channel to England, but he was determined to stop the English getting too powerful and too rich so he tried to stop them sending ships to Egypt to sell English goods.

He took his army to Egypt and he also took a group of historians and scientists so that they could explore the ruins of Ancient Egypt. In 1798 Napoleon conquered Egypt, but the English navy, led by Admiral Nelson, destroyed the French ships at the mouth of the River Nile. In 1799 Napoleon returned to France, leaving his army behind to fight the English on land.

Two hundred years ago, in 1799, the most important clue to the mystery of the hieroglyphs was found in Egypt. It was a huge block of greyish stone with signs all over one side of it. It was found in a place called Rashid, or Rosetta, near where the River Nile flows into the sea. (Look at the map on page 12 to find Rosetta.) There are two stories about how it was found. One of them says that it was part of a stone wall which some French soldiers – who were in Napoleon's army in Egypt – had been ordered to pull down so that they could build a fort. The second story says that it was just found on the ground.

The soldier who found the Rosetta Stone was called Lieutenant Pierre François Xavier Bouchard. He saw the Greek writing and realized straight away that the other signs on the Stone were in Egyptian **script**. He thought that the Egyptian writing might say the same as the Greek writing. He reported the find to his general in the army, General Menou.

The Stone was put in safekeeping in Cairo. The scientists and **historians** who had gone to Egypt with Napoleon were very excited about the find. They translated the Greek section easily, because most scholars at that time had learned **Latin** and **Greek** at school. The difficult part was the writing on the other part of the Stone. The Greek section said that the other two sections repeated what was said in the Greek writing, but still nobody could work out how to read them. So the **scholars** in Cairo made copies of the Stone to send to other scholars around Europe who were already studying Ancient Egyptian scripts.

How do you think these copies were made? First, two men covered the surface of the Stone with a very dark black ink called printer's ink. Then they put a sheet of paper over the ink and rolled it with rubber rollers until they got a clear print. It worked in the same way that potato prints work. Why didn't the scholars just take a photograph of the Stone?

Napoleon's troops parading at Rosetta in 1799. This engraving comes from an original picture by a French artist, Dominique Vivant Denon.

POTATO PRINTS

Have you ever made potato prints? If you have then you'll know that the bits you have cut out of the potato, like the signs carved out of the stone, are left white on the paper while the rest of the paper takes on the colour you've painted the parts left sticking out of the potato.

On 15 September 1799, a report about the discovery of the Rosetta Stone was sent from Cairo to Paris. The news spread from there to Egyptologists (the scholars who study Ancient Egypt) in France, Sweden, Germany – and England. Two years later, a troop of English soldiers was sent to Egypt to attack Napoleon's forces. The English General knew that the French had the Stone in their possession and he was determined to capture it and take it back to England!

General Menou had taken the Stone to Alexandria. It was hidden in his house. He thought it might be safe from the English there, but he was wrong. The English troops defeated the French, and an English officer, Major-General Turner, went to Alexandria to claim the Stone as part of the agreement made between the English and the French after the fighting. General Menou said the Stone was his own private property, but Major-General Turner said that it was not. General Menou was forced to agree to give it up. The story goes that a French officer handed over the Stone to a group of English soldiers. He warned them to get it out of Alexandria as quickly as possible, before anybody discovered what had happened.

The Rosetta Stone newly cleaned in 1999, showing its original colour.

Would it have been easy to get the Stone out of its hiding place and hand it over to the English? How heavy do you think it is?

Why do you think the French general was so keen to keep the Stone? And why do you think the English were so keen to have it in England?

If you ever see the real Stone, look very carefully at the left-hand side and you can see, in faded writing, 'CAPTURED IN EGYPT BY THE BRITISH ARMY IN 1801'.

Egyptian sculptures being installed → in the British Museum.

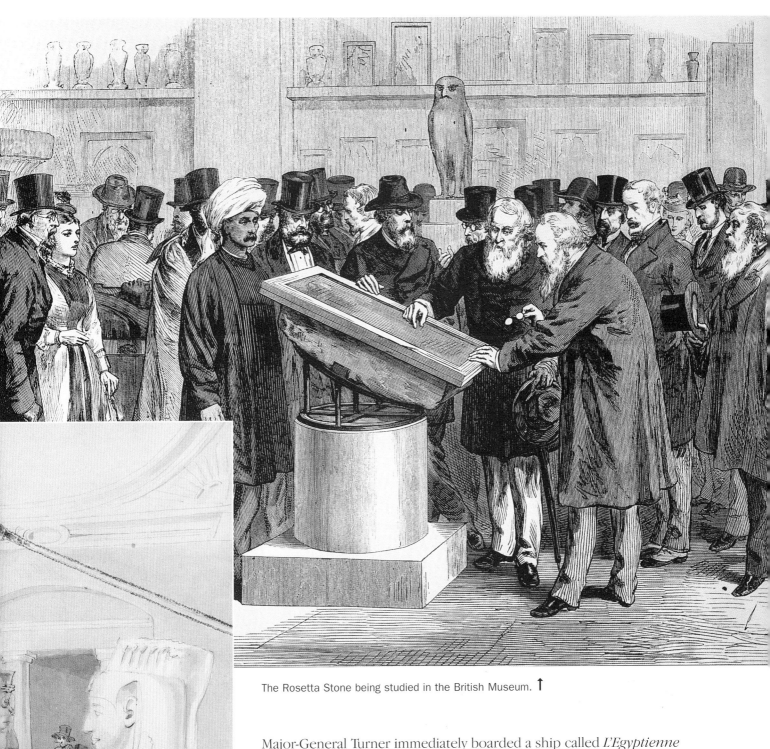

The Rosetta Stone being studied in the British Museum. ↑

Major-General Turner immediately boarded a ship called *L'Egyptienne* with the Stone. He arrived in Portsmouth with it in February 1802. There was great excitement when it arrived in London and, almost immediately, four plaster casts were made of it. One was sent to Oxford University, one was sent to Cambridge University, one was sent to Edinburgh University and the fourth one was sent to Trinity College in Dublin. Why do you think that was done?

Finally, at the end of 1802, the Stone was taken to the British Museum, where it has been ever since. How many years has it been there?

THOMAS YOUNG

Thomas Young.

One of the many scholars who were excited by the news of the arrival of the Rosetta Stone in England was an extraordinarily clever man called Thomas Young. He was born in Somerset in 1773 and he could read by the time he was two years old. By the time he was seven he had learned **Latin** and Greek, and by the time he was twelve he could also speak **Hebrew** and Persian. At fourteen, he could speak Arabic, French, Italian and Spanish.

Thomas Young went on to study medicine and was particularly interested in how eyes worked. That led him to do experiments with light, and he eventually wrote a book which is studied by physicists even now. It is called *The Undulatory Theory of Light.* It is said that he played the flute and could dance very well. So, you see, he was not only interested in everything, but also very clever at whatever he took an interest in.

When Thomas Young was already well known as a doctor and as a physicist, he began to turn his attention to the mystery of the hieroglyphs.

He must have heard from other scholars about the arrival of the Rosetta Stone in England, but he did not see it or a copy of it to begin with. By this time, travellers to Egypt were taking treasures of all kinds from the temples and tombs which they visited. At that time no-one thought it was wrong to do that. In 1814, Thomas Young got a copy of the Rosetta Stone's inscriptions. The same year a friend brought him a roll of papyrus from Egypt which was covered in demotic writing, and that seems to have inspired him to try to succeed in solving the mystery which had baffled everybody else before him. Thomas Young proudly said that it would take him no time at all to **translate** the signs on the papyrus, and then he would go on to decipher the demotic section of the Rosetta Stone, and then the hieroglyphic section. He clearly was not used to failing in anything he decided to do!

First, Thomas Young sent a letter to the Swedish scholar, Johann David Åkerblad. Young asked him how far he had managed to get in finding out what some of the signs meant. Åkerblad kindly sent Young the results of all his work. You will remember that Åkerblad knew Coptic, and that had helped him to guess what some of the signs might mean. Thomas Young knew a lot of languages, but he had not learned Coptic. How did he think that he would manage to get any further with solving the mystery if he did not understand what the words meant?

Thomas Young started with the signs in the words that Åkerblad had found – in particular the names of people and places – and so he already had a list of words to work with. He then began to look at his copy of the Rosetta Stone and to count how many times certain words appeared in the Greek section. (Remember that he had learned Greek, so he was able to translate those words into English.) The next step was to find a group of signs in the demotic section which appeared the same number of times. He found that the same group of signs could be found on almost every line. He guessed that would be the Egyptian for ... which word?

Which word do you think you would find most often in a piece of English writing? Have a look at this page and see whether you can see which word is used the most times.

First, Thomas Young sent a letter to **the** Swedish schola
Åkerblad. Young asked him how far he had managed to
what some of **the** signs meant. Åkerblad kindly sent Yo
all his work. You will remember that Åkerblad knew Co
helped him to guess what some of **the** signs might me
knew a lot of languages, but he had not learned Coptic
that he would manage to get any further with solving
did not understand what **the** words meant?

Thomas Young started with **the** signs in **the** words th
found – in particular **the** names of people and place
had a list of words to work with. He then began to lo
the Rosetta Stone and to count how many times ce
in **the** Greek section. (Remember that he had learn
Greek, so he was able
to translate those
words into English.)
The next step was to
find a group of signs in
the demotic section
which appeared **the**
same number of times.
He found that **the** same
group of signs could be
found on almost every
line. He guessed that
would be **the** Egyptian
for ... which word?

Which word do you think
you would find most
often in a piece of English
writing? Have a look at this
page and see whether you
can see which word is used
the most times.

26

After that Thomas Young looked at other words which he could understand in Greek, counted how many times they were in the Greek section, and then again looked for groups of signs which occurred the same number of times in the demotic section. In this way he built up a much longer list of signs he could recognize than Johann David Åkerblad had managed to do.

But Thomas Young had two problems with this way of working. One of them was that the demotic section of the Stone was broken at the edge, like a page of a book which has been torn, so the writing was not complete. The other was that the Greek section and the demotic section were not exactly the same, word for word. That meant that Thomas Young made some mistakes in his translation.

He then turned his attention to the hieroglyphic section. The most important step forward he made was to decide that the demotic section was really another way of writing the hieroglyphic section.

PHONOGRAMS

You will remember that phonograms are signs which stand for sounds. For example, 'l' stands for the sound at the beginning and end of 'level'.

The next step in solving the mystery was to decide whether all the hieroglyphs stood for sounds – like the English alphabet – or whether some of them stood for objects or ideas. You will remember that a hundred years earlier Jean Jacques Barthelemy had decided that the names of people in the hieroglyphs were surrounded by 'cartouches', so Thomas Young looked for the cartouches in the hieroglyphic section of the Stone. It so happened that there were six cartouches. Three of them were quite short, like this:

Three were longer, like this:

Have a good look at the two cartouches. What can you see? Have you noticed that the longer one starts with the same hieroglyphs as the short one?

Thomas knew that in the demotic script some signs stood for sounds – they were phonograms.

Using the signs he knew already and guessing that the name of the king was PTOLEMY he worked out that the short cartouche spelled out PTOLEMAIOS (the Greek spelling of Ptolemy) and that the extra signs in the longer cartouche meant 'May he live forever beloved of Ptah'.

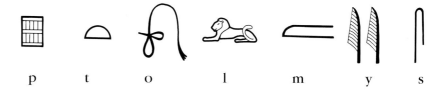

| p | t | o | l | m | y | s |

He then found another cartouche in a copy of some hieroglyphs written on the walls of the temple at Karnak. (Look at the map on page 12 to find Karnak.) He went through the same process as before and recognized the Greek name of a queen called Berenice.

Cartouche of Berenice

28

Young worked out that the last hieroglyph was not a phonogram but just showed that the name was female. Signs like this are now called 'determinatives'. Do we have determinatives in the English alphabet?

PTAH

Ptah was one of the most important Ancient Egyptian gods. In Egyptian writing he is described as 'creator of the earth, father of the gods and all the beings of this earth, father of beginnings'. His name in hieroglyphs looks like this:

DETERMINATIVE

A determinative is a hieroglyphic sign which explains what kind of word you are reading. It has no sound. It is always placed at the end of a word.

Thomas Young made some small mistakes, but he did get quite a lot right. How many hieroglyphs do you know now? Could you write your name with them?

In a very short space of time, Thomas Young had discovered a lot about hieroglyphs. He had found that some of the signs in cartouches stood for sounds. He had found that some signs just gave the reader more information about the word which had been written, and did not stand either for a sound or an object. He had found that it was possible to guess the meaning of some of the hieroglyphs by counting how often they were to be found in the writing. He also had understood that the demotic script was a kind of handwritten version of hieroglyphic script.

Having gone that far with his discovery he began to slow down – and finally came to a stop! Like all the scholars before him he still believed that apart from the Greek names in the cartouches and a few other words, most of the hieroglyphs were symbols (pictures) and their meaning was only known to the Ancient Egyptian priests. He thought it would be impossible ever to read all of them or to make any sense out of them.

He **published** what he had discovered in the *Encyclopaedia Britannica* of 1819. (Do you have an encyclopaedia at school or at home? Maybe it is the *Encyclopaedia Britannica*. Find out in which year it was published.) He also wrote a letter to a young Frenchman called Jean François Champollion, who had a particular interest in the Rosetta Stone. What Thomas Young did not know was how keen Champollion was to be the first person to break the code and make it possible to read all about Ancient Egypt.

The god Ptah and his wife Sekhmet.

JEAN FRANÇOIS CHAMPOLLION

Jean-François Champollion, ↑
painted by Coignet.

In 1790, seventeen years after Thomas Young was born in England, a baby was born in France. His name was Jean François Champollion and he was the fifth child in his family. They lived in a town called Figeac in the South of France. Their house is still there today.

His father, Jacques Champollion, sold books and the house must have been full of books, old and new. Jean François began to read at a very early age. He was taught by his brother who was twelve years older than him. His brother's name was Jacques Joseph.

Jacques Joseph was very excited by the news that his hero, Napoleon, was going to lead an expedition to Egypt. He would have dearly liked to go on that expedition, but he was too young. He had read as much as he could about Egypt in the books that his father brought into the house. He had also seen in the newspapers that Napoleon was going to take with him scientists and **historians** to explore the ruins of Ancient Egypt. Jacques Joseph talked to his younger brother, Jean François, about the pyramids and the temples and the mummies, and showed him drawings which had been made by travellers to Egypt.

The Champollion family's house at Figeac. →
It is now a museum.

Jacques Joseph Champollion

When Jean François was eight his father sent him to school. Jacques Joseph had left home to work in a city called Grenoble, so he could no longer teach Jean François. Then three years later his father decided to send him to join his brother in Grenoble. At the age of eleven, he set off on his own in a coach pulled by horses on the long journey to the city.

When he arrived in Grenoble, Jean Jacques arranged for him to go to school. Jean François hated being at school and sent his brother long letters complaining about how unhappy he was. He sent letters to his brother for the rest of his life. His brother kept them, and much later they were published in a book – that is how we know so much about what Jean François was thinking and what he was doing.

Although he could not be bothered to learn mathematics or science, he worked hard at learning Latin and Greek, and he even learned Arabic and Coptic and other ancient languages. Like his brother, he was very excited about what he had heard and read about Ancient Egypt, and he knew that if he learned Coptic he might be learning what the Ancient Egyptian language sounded like. So he spent all his free time at school studying languages, which none of the other boys could understand. He was so good at languages that before he finally left school at sixteen, he stood up at the prize-giving ceremony and recited verses from the Old Testament of the Bible in **Hebrew.**

Meanwhile Jacques Joseph had already seen a copy of the Rosetta Stone. He had become a librarian in Grenoble and was still deeply interested in Ancient Egypt. He translated the Greek section of the Rosetta Stone and must have told his younger brother all about what he was doing.

The next year, 1807, the Champollion brothers went to Paris. Jean François became a student and soon, even though he was only seventeen, the historians and the archaeologists he met realized how much he knew about ancient languages and how keen he was to learn more. Imagine his excitement when an **archaeologist** gave him a print of all the writing on the Rosetta Stone!

From that day on, Jean François Champollion tried and tried again to solve the mystery of the hieroglyphs.

SUCCESS AT LAST

On 14 September 1822, Jean François Champollion sat down at his desk up in the attic of a tall house in Paris. He had been working very hard in the years since he had arrived in the city, but he had still not managed to decipher more than the thirteen characters in the names Ptolemy and Cleopatra. He was sure he had managed to read those hieroglyphs correctly because they stood for sounds and he already knew the two names. All the other hieroglyphs, when they were not used for Greek names, he thought stood for ideas. He had read what Thomas Young had written, but he still believed that most of the hieroglyphs stood for ideas; that was why it was so difficult to understand them.

He was beginning to give up hope. Would Thomas Young win the race after all? Why, he, Jean François Champollion of Figeac, had been trying to understand the Rosetta Stone ever since he'd received a copy of it fourteen years ago. Thomas Young had already published his findings three years before!

But today he had something new to look at. A friend of his, who was a **professor** of architecture, had travelled to Egypt and had gone by boat along the Nile as far as the huge temples of Abu Simbel. There he had carefully copied some of the hieroglyphs which cover the walls of the temples. You can still see them there if you go to Egypt today. He had taken particular care to copy the hieroglyphs which were surrounded by cartouches.

When the architect got back to Paris he took his drawings to Jean François, who started to look through the sheets of paper. 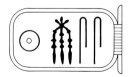 Suddenly, his eyes were caught by one cartouche which he had never seen before, but which he realized he could read.

Rameses II

He used his knowledge of Coptic and of the thirteen characters he knew already, and discovered that the name in front of him was RAMESES, the famous Pharaoh who had built the temples at Abu Simbel. If an Egyptian name, Rameses, was written in phonograms, then all of the Egyptian language might be written that way too.

He could hardly go on. Was he really about to break the code? He had just discovered that he had been wrong in thinking that the hieroglyphs only stood for ideas. Instead, he realized that the hieroglyphs which had been used to write the name of the Pharaoh Rameses stood for sounds. If that was really true, then he would be able to build up an alphabet by translating all the cartouches he could find, and working out which sound each hieroglyph stood for. Then he could read all the other Egyptian texts.

Would he manage to translate another name? He could hardly breathe in his excitement. This time he chose a cartouche which began with a hieroglyph in the shape of an ibis, like this:

He knew that the ibis stood for the Egyptian god called Thoth. He also knew that the second sign stood for 'm', and that the third sign stood for 's', as in Rameses. So he had read THOTMOS – or Thutmose, which was the name of another Pharaoh. He had done it by using his knowledge of Coptic, his knowledge of the names of the Pharaohs, and the hieroglyphs which he had already found in other names.

He had to tell his brother. He rushed down the narrow staircase, ran to the library where Jacques Joseph worked, burst into his office, and shouted 'I've done it! I've done it!' Then, according to his brother's son who wrote about it later, he fell to the ground in a deep faint.

CHAMPOLLION GOES TO EGYPT

Suddenly, Jean François Champollion became famous. He was the envy of all the other **scholars** who had wanted to be the first to understand the meaning of the hieroglyphs on the Rosetta Stone. He was invited to explain his discovery to the most important historians and scholars in Paris. He was taken to meet Louis XVIII, the King of France. The King gave him enough money to travel to Italy. Now he could visit the collections of statues, rolls of papyrus, and mummies which Italian travellers had brought back from the ruins of the temples and the pyramids of Ancient Egypt and put into their museums or their homes.

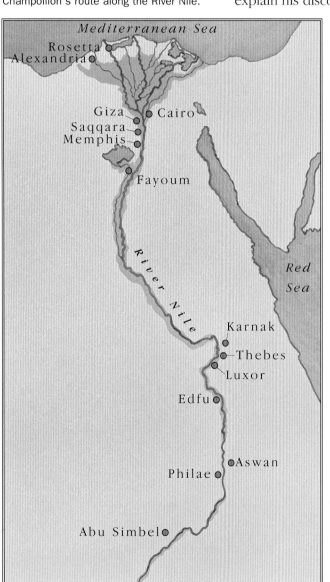

Champollion's route along the River Nile.

More and more people were collecting the treasures of Ancient Egypt to take back to their own countries. Huge columns covered in hieroglyphs, statues of gods and goddesses, jewellery, mummy cases covered in highly-coloured pictures – the collectors took anything which could possibly be carried across the desert and then shipped across the sea.

In the city of Turin in Italy you can still see a collection which Jean François Champollion went to visit.

Jean François Champollion spent a long time in Turin. Now, instead of studying the drawings or prints of these beautiful objects as he had done in France, he was able to look at the real things. He found a room in the museum in Turin with a huge pile of papyrus rolls. They were beginning to turn to dust. The brightly coloured pictures were fading and the writing was becoming difficult to read. He was shocked! He arranged for the rolls to be stored so that the papyrus did not get too dry, and he slowly read the writing on them, translating the signs into French after he had worked out what sounds they stood for.

Also in Italy was a large collection which an Englishman called Henry Salt had brought back from Egypt by boat to an Italian port called Livorno. Jean François desperately wanted to buy all the beautiful statues of Egyptian gods and blocks of stone covered in hieroglyphs and have them carried back to Paris to put in what is now the famous museum called the Louvre. Finally, he persuaded the French King to buy the collection and it was transported by sea from Livorno to the French harbour called Le Havre, and from there up the River Seine to Paris. You can imagine how excited Jean François was to be able to show Parisians the amazing treasures of Ancient Egypt. He became the **curator** of the Egyptian Museum of the Louvre in 1826, and now, 170 years later, people can still go and visit that same collection.

Although Jean François loved travelling to Italy, his dream was that he too would go to Egypt and see for himself the country which he had only read about and heard about. He could not wait to find out if the way he had read the hieroglyphs on the Rosetta Stone would mean that he could read all that was written on the temple walls and the pyramids. If he had worked it out correctly, then all the mysteries of how the Ancient Egyptians lived and what they believed in would become clear to him!

Finally, in 1828, with the help of a rich friend, he had enough money to get together a small group of French and Italian scholars and to set off by ship to the Egyptian port of Alexandria. From there, the scholars and some Egyptian sailors boarded two long boats called 'dahabieh' and started the long journey up the River Nile. You can see on the map all the places they visited. As they slowly sailed past great pyramids and ancient temples, Jean François was so excited by what he saw that he did not notice the terrible heat or that he was ill because of bad food. Now, at last, he could look at hieroglyphs in the temples which were still standing, on great columns and on mummy cases, just as they had first been written.

Whenever the boats came to a place along the Nile where there had been a port or a town in Ancient Egypt, they tied up to the bank of the river and spent days exploring the ruins. One or two of the group would make drawings of the pictures and Jean François would use the dictionary of hieroglyphs he was writing to read what was carved around the pictures. Here is a page of a book, which he wrote using the notes he made as they slowly sailed down the Nile.

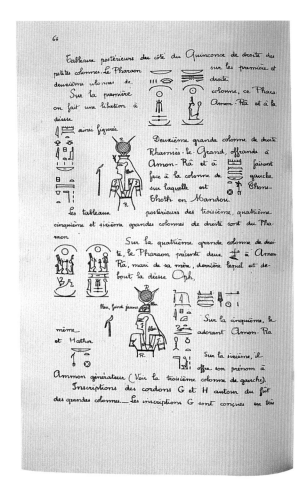

In English his notes mean, 'On the fourth big column on the right, the Pharaoh presents two (gifts?) to Amon Ra, husband of his mother, behind whom stands the goddess Oph'. On the picture of the god below you can see that Jean François has noted which colours are used for each part. 'Bleu' means blue, 'j' stands for 'jaune' (yellow), and 'r' stands for 'rouge' (red).

In this book, Jean François described every detail of the writing and the pictures and all the temples he explored. You can imagine what hard work it was, and how long it took for the little group of scholars to record all that they saw. It was very hot, there were sandstorms, and sometimes they had very little food to eat, because they were often far away from where people were living.

We know what happened on his journey along the Nile because of the letters Jean François Champollion wrote to his brother. The letters tell how on 26 December 1828 the two boats reached Abu Simbel ... There, just ahead of them across the sand, were two temples. Jean François had heard all about them from the friend who had brought him the drawings of the cartouches, and he had read descriptions of them written by travellers, but he had not expected to find such an amazing sight. One temple had been built to honour King Rameses II and the other was for his Queen, Nefertari. The temples had huge statues of the King and Queen carved out of the rock on the outside walls. They had been built so that when the sun rose in the early morning, it shone on the faces of the statues and lit them up, turning their colour from a deep grey-red to orange-yellow. Although Jean François was very excited by the beauty of the temples, he decided to explore them thoroughly on the return journey. So they continued on to Wadi Halfa, the final stop on the journey south.

On New Year's Day 1829 the two boats turned north. There was a very strong wind blowing. The oarsmen could hardly keep the boats on course and Jean François was sick because the water was so rough. Finally they tied up alongside the riverbank at Abu Simbel. But poor Jean François had to wait three days until he could explore the temples. He was ill with gout, which meant that he had a dreadful pain in his knee, so bad that he could not walk. He had to watch from the boat while the rest of the group disappeared through the entrance to the temple, climbing up and over the top of the sand hill which the wind had blown over the feet of the enormous seated figures.

Abu Simbel today.

Jean François did not wait until he was really better. He was too impatient. With two Egyptian oarsmen to support him, he limped painfully across the short distance between the boat and the temple. He rested for a few minutes near the statue on the left of the entrance and then, just before going in through the doorway, he stripped off all his clothes, except for a shirt, a pair of underpants and some long woollen socks. It was going to be very hot inside and he wanted to stay there as long as he could. There was a lot to do.

All the walls were covered with hieroglyphs, some of them carved right up to the ceiling, so high that he had to use a ladder to get close enough to see them. Using his dictionary he read one group of hieroglyphs which described how a messenger had announced to Rameses that the enemy had attacked his soldiers and how the war chariot had been prepared so that the King could lead his army into battle. Slowly and painfully, in the tremendous heat, Jean François dragged himself along the lines of writing. He made notes as he went. There were long stories about the battles fought by Rameses and all the victories he had won.

A painting of Champollion and his friends in Arab clothes. The artist was one of the Italians who went to Egypt with him.

Finally, after three hours, Jean François could work no more. With the help of his two Egyptian friends he made his way back to the entrance and out into the freezing cold wind of the desert. He quickly put on all his clothes – a shirt, two flannel waistcoats, a coat, a cloak and woollen trousers held up with a wide belt. Then he limped back to the boat and stretched out on his bunk. The pain in his knee did not matter; his mind was full of the stories he had read about Rameses. Now, at last, by using his dictionary of hieroglyphs, the whole world would be able to know what had happened thousands of years ago!

And so he and his Italian and French friends worked on in the heat of the temples for the next five days, some of them making careful drawings of each wall, some taking rubbings of the writing by covering it with paper and shading over the carved letters. Jean François chose what he needed to be copied and told the others what to do. There was too much for him to translate while he was there in the temple, and he decided to take the copies back to France and work on them later.

On 16 January, he gave the order to set sail once again. On they went along the Nile, stopping to carry on the work of copying what they found in the ruins along the banks.

Jean François spent almost another year in Egypt before he returned to France. By the time he arrived back in Paris he was very ill. But there was still work for him to do. He wanted to finish writing his dictionary of hieroglyphs. Also, now he understood what the words meant, he could write a book of grammar to show how the language worked.

Here is a page from his dictionary.

Here is a page from the book of grammar he wrote.

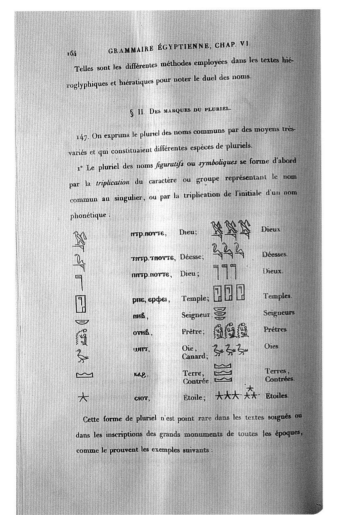

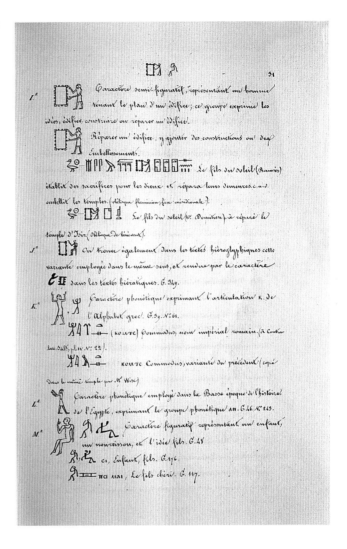

The text on this page says, 'this page explains how singular nouns are turned into the plural'. You will see that the first sign in the list, which means 'god', is used three times to make it become 'gods' and every sign down the list is repeated three times to turn it into the plural. The signs mean god/goddess, temple, lord, priest, goose/duck, land/country.
Can you guess the last one?

Jean François Champollion died in 1832. He was only 42 years old. His brother, Jean Jacques, made sure that all his writing was published so that everybody in future who wanted to read for themselves the stories of Ancient Egypt, could learn how to decipher hieroglyphs. In the next chapter of this book you will begin to learn how to read them too!

READING
HIEROGLYPHS

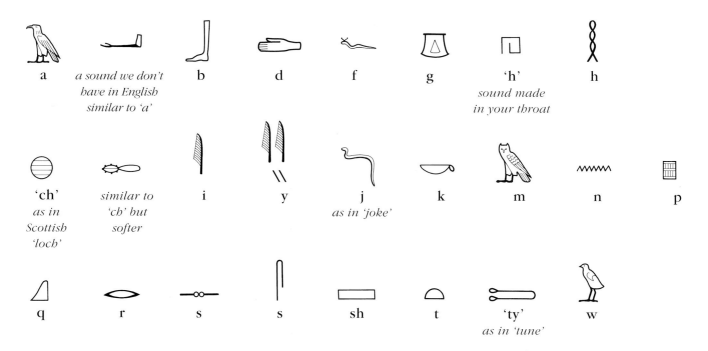

a	*a sound we don't have in English similar to 'a'*	**b**	**d**	**f**	**g**	**'h'** *sound made in your throat*	**h**

'ch' *as in Scottish 'loch'*	*similar to 'ch' but softer*	**i**	**y**	**j** *as in 'joke'*	**k**	**m**	**n**	**p**

q	**r**	**s**	**s**	**sh**	**t**	**'ty'** *as in 'tune'*	**w**

Here is a list of twenty-five hieroglyphs. Each sign stands for a single sound.

Using these sounds, can you write your whole name in hieroglyphs? Why not? You might remember that on page 18 you read that the Ancient Egyptians did not have signs for all the **vowel** sounds we use. So now try to write your name without all the vowels in it.

Now that you have tried to copy the hieroglyphs, you will realize that some of them look exactly like an object, but that others are not like anything you can recognize. For instance:

looks exactly like a foot,

and looks exactly like a snake, but

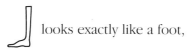 only looks like a garden pool when we have been told that is what it is meant to look like.

Remember that this list of hieroglyphs is a list of phonograms (you found out what phonograms were on page 17). Even if they look like objects, here they are used to stand for sounds, not things.

Some hieroglyphs stand for two or even three sounds. Here are some examples, with their meanings:

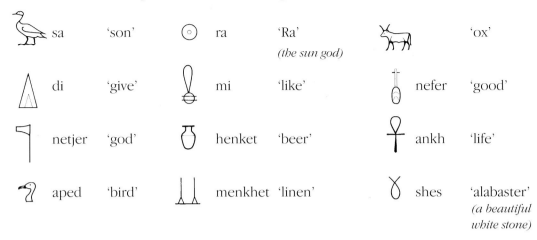

sa	'son'	ra	'Ra' *(the sun god)*		'ox'		
di	'give'	mi	'like'	nefer	'good'		
netjer	'god'	henket	'beer'	ankh	'life'		
aped	'bird'	menkhet	'linen'	shes	'alabaster' *(a beautiful white stone)*		

And then there are the hieroglyphs which are called 'determinatives' (remember, you first heard about these on pages 16-17), because they help the reader decide what the group of hieroglyphs standing before them really means. For instance:

This logogram shows a scribe's tools: an ink palette with a water bottle and a brush.

When it has the determinative showing a man, it means 'scribe'.

When it is written like this with a papyrus roll determinative, it means 'writing'. (Do you remember what a logogram is? See page 17.)

INSCRIPTION

An inscription is a piece of writing which is 'inscribed', or carved, on to a stone monument, or a coin, or a medal. Temples and tombs in Ancient Egypt were covered with inscriptions.

To show that a group of signs spelt out a name, the Egyptians put a little figure of a person as a determinative at the end. So, to write your name in Egyptian properly, you should finish it off with a little woman if you are a girl or a little man if you are a boy.

Let's look at a line of hieroglyphs which is taken from an inscription.

You will notice that all the animals and birds are facing the same way. That was the scribe's way of showing the reader where to start reading. They are facing towards the beginning of the line and so the reader needs to read the line from left to right.

Another one of the difficulties about trying to read hieroglyphs is that they aren't always written in straight lines like our writing. They are sometimes fitted in around a big picture. Here is a picture with writing around it.

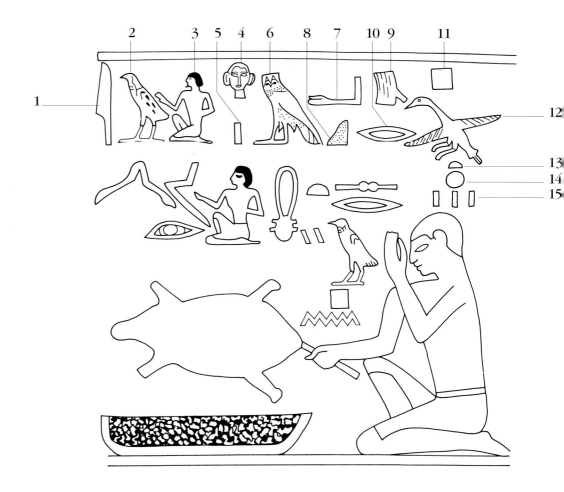

The numbers have been put in to show you the order in which you have to read the first sentence of hieroglyphs. The whole inscription means 'I have been roasting since the beginning of time – I have never seen the like of this goose'.

Numbers are useful for keeping records and writing lists of things. Egyptian numbers are very easy to read and write. Numbers up to 10 were written with strokes, like this:

I	II	III	II II	III II	III III	IIII III	IIII IIII	IIIII IIII
1	2	3	4	5	6	7	8	9

10 is written ∩ , 100 ℰ and 1,000 ⚲

Lots of Egyptian tombs contained lists of all the things the dead person wanted to take to the afterlife. Egyptologists call these 'offering stelae' (a stele is a carved slab of stone). If you go to a museum with an Egyptian collection, you can probably find one to look at.

Here is part of an offering stele in the British Museum. The stele belonged to a man called Rahotep. It shows him sitting at a table enjoying food and drink in the afterlife. Look at the writing under the table. You should be able to work out some of the signs. The writing is a list of some of the things Rahotep wanted for the afterlife. How many of each thing did he want? The answer is on page 44.

If you do visit a museum, you will find lots of statues and carvings of Egypt's kings. If you look at them carefully you will often find the king's name written on them. The Egyptians had many words for 'king'. Here are two of them:

 nisut   bity

The king was the most important person in ancient Egypt and had lots of titles. His two most important titles were:

 nisut   bity 'The Dual King'

and

 sa   ra 'Son of Ra'.

Next to the titles or underneath them, the king's names were written inside cartouches. (You read about cartouches on page 16.) Here are the names and titles of some famous kings:

Thutmose III

Rameses II

Tutankhamun

The Egyptians thought their kings were gods who brought life to their people, so in front of or above the king's name you will sometimes find:

 netjer nefer 'The Good God'

and after it:

 di ankh 'who gives life'.

Now you know some hieroglyphs, you can use them to write secret messages to your friends by spelling words out with the one-sound signs. Sometimes you might need to invent your own signs for things. Scribes in ancient Egypt had to do this when new things were invented - like chariots. How would you write 'car' or 'plane'?

You might want to learn more about how to read hieroglyphs. If so, there are lots of books which will help you, but it is hard work! Despite everything that Champollion and later scholars did, we are still a long way from understanding all the mysteries of the hieroglyphs.

Perhaps you might want to look at other kinds of writing from different parts of the world. Some scripts – such as one from Crete called Linear B – have taken scholars a very long time to decipher and the story of how it happened is as exciting as the story of the Rosetta Stone. There is another script from northern India called the Indus Valley script which nobody has yet discovered how to read. Maybe you will manage it one day!

(Answer: The things Rahotep wanted are: alabaster, bread, linen (clothing) and beer. He wanted a thousand of each thing.)

FURTHER READING

For children

British Museum Incredible Writing Box
(British Museum Press, 1998)

Judith Crosher,
See Through History: Ancient Egypt
(Hamlyn, 1995)

Pam Harper,
Writing Activity Book
(British Museum Press, 1996)

Geraldine Harris and Delia Pemberton,
British Museum Illustrated Encyclopaedia of Ancient Egypt
(British Museum Press, 1999)

Jane Shuter,
The Ancient World: Egypt
(Wayland, 1998)

For adults

Mark Collier and Bill Manley,
How to Read Egyptian Hieroglyphs
(British Museum Press, 1998)

W. V. Davies,
Reading the Past: Egyptian Hieroglyphs
(British Museum Press, 1987)

Vivian Davies and Renée Friedman,
Egypt
(British Museum Press, 1998)

Ian Shaw and Paul Nicholson,
British Museum Dictionary of Ancient Egypt
(British Museum Press, 1995)

GLOSSARY

WORDS TO DO WITH LANGUAGE

consonant   a letter of the alphabet – for example, b, c, d , f, g – which is used with vowels to make a word. (See also vowel). You use your lips or your tongue to make the sound of a consonant.

decipher   to work out how to read something which is difficult to read, such as a code.

Greek   the language spoken in Greece.

Hebrew   the language spoken in the country now known as Israel. The Old Testament of the Bible was written in Hebrew.

Latin   the language spoken by the Romans in Italy and in the Roman Empire.

(These three languages were spoken by people in ancient times. They have changed over the hundreds of years since then. Modern Greek and modern Hebrew are different from Ancient Greek and Ancient Hebrew, and Latin became modern Italian.)

publish   to prepare and print a writer's book so that other people can read it.

script   any particular type of writing.

translate   to write or speak something written or said in one language in another language.
For example, you might translate something written in French into English so that English people can understand what it says

vowel	the five letters a, e, i, o, u are the only vowels in the alphabet. They are each used on their own or with other vowels and with a consonant or a group of consonants to make a word. You make a vowel sound in your throat without using your tongue.

WORDS TO DO WITH PEOPLE

archaeologist	someone who looks at the remains of the past – for example, ancient buildings, tombs, or pottery – to find out more about how people lived in the past.
curator	the person in charge of the exhibitions in a museum or art gallery.
historian	someone who studies the past and often writes about it.
priest	a religious person who leads other people in their worship of the god or gods who they believe in.
physicist	a scientist who is particularly interested in how the world works and in finding answers to questions like 'Why does a ball fall down when you drop it?'
professor	somebody who studies a subject and writes about it, and teaches students about it in a university.
scholar	a person who spends his or her life studying a subject and is very clever.
sculptor	an artist who works in stone or metal or wood.

INDEX